YOUR KNOWLEDGE HAS VALUE

- We will publish your bachelor's and master's thesis, essays and papers

- Your own eBook and book - sold worldwide in all relevant shops

- Earn money with each sale

Upload your text at www.GRIN.com and publish for free

Bibliographic information published by the German National Library:

The German National Library lists this publication in the National Bibliography; detailed bibliographic data are available on the Internet at http://dnb.dnb.de .

This book is copyright material and must not be copied, reproduced, transferred, distributed, leased, licensed or publicly performed or used in any way except as specifically permitted in writing by the publishers, as allowed under the terms and conditions under which it was purchased or as strictly permitted by applicable copyright law. Any unauthorized distribution or use of this text may be a direct infringement of the author s and publisher s rights and those responsible may be liable in law accordingly.

Imprint:

Copyright © 2014 GRIN Verlag
Print and binding: Books on Demand GmbH, Norderstedt Germany
ISBN: 9783668659612

This book at GRIN:

https://www.grin.com/document/416097

Peter Krause

Commentary on Irshad al-Fusuk uka tahqiq al-haqq min 'ilm al-usul by Al-Shawkani

GRIN Verlag

GRIN - Your knowledge has value

Since its foundation in 1998, GRIN has specialized in publishing academic texts by students, college teachers and other academics as e-book and printed book. The website www.grin.com is an ideal platform for presenting term papers, final papers, scientific essays, dissertations and specialist books.

Visit us on the internet:

http://www.grin.com/

http://www.facebook.com/grincom

http://www.twitter.com/grin_com

Commentary on:

Irshād al-Fuṣūl ilā tahqīq al-ḥaqq min ʿilm al-uṣūl by Al-Shawkānī
(Text B)

word count: 1972

Islamic Law and Society

21 November 2014 – Exeter

The text "*Irshād al-Fuhūl ilā tahqīq al-haqq min 'ilm al-uṣūl*" is written by Muhammad 'Alī b. Muhammad Al-Shawkānī. He is a Sunnī legal scholar, writer and teacher from Yemen,[1] who lived from 1760 until 1839.[2] Al-Shawkānī is seen as one of the most influential modern Islamic jurists, which is supported by the qualification of him as '*mudjaddid*' or 'regenerator' by Ra<u>sh</u>īd Riḍā.[3] Al-Shawkānī achieved a good reputation by working on defining requirements to attain the different status as a jurist.[4] He is described as "an ardent opponent on the restrictions of *ijmā'*" and known "for his support for the greater use of the *ijtihād*".[5] This text fits in his released literature about the requirements of attaining different levels of legal scholarship. Roughly translated, the title means: "Guideline for the experts to achieve the truth in the science of the principles of the law". Al-Shawkānī gives in his text basic conditions, which are required to be a *mujtahid*.

In my opinion a *mujtahid* is a Muslim jurist, who has the ability to perform *ijtihād*. Al-Shawkānī specifies what a *mujtahid* is in paragraph two. In his opinion, a *mujtahid* must try to acquire an opinion of a legal rule and have the ability to derive legal rules by working with the legal sources. Obligatory for this are adulthood and sanity. After this section, he starts listing the conditions, but obviously, adulthood and sanity are also requirements to be a *mujtahid*. The difference to the following conditions is, that this inherent quality can not be changed by the prospective *mujtahid* in contrast to the following acquirable

---

1 J Jansen, "Al-Shawkānī, Muhammad b. 'Alī", *Encyclopaedia of Islam: Second Edition,* IX, p.378
2 G Kramer, "Islam and the Muslim world: Political Islam", in *Encyclopedia of Islam and the Muslim World*, Vol.2, p.536
3 J Jansen, *loc. cit.,* p.378
4 B Haykel, "*Revival and Reform in Islam: The Legacy of Muhammad al-Shawkānī*" (2003), p.76-7
5 K Vikor, *'Between God and the Sultan: A History of Islamic Law'* (2005), p.123

conditions.

The first acquirable condition is that a *mujtahid* must know the primary texts of Islamic Law.[6] Al-Shawkānī builds up a progressive reasoning starting from the general point that a *mujtahid* does not have to know all of the *Qur'an* and the *Sunnah* and goes on to discuss what is necessary to know. He disagrees with the legal scholars Ghazālī and Ibn al-'Arabī, criticising that 500 verses of the *Qur'an* are too little knowledge.[7] Al-Shawkānī asserts that a *mujtahid* with good understanding of the texts can extract legal rules from more than 500 verses by working on implications or consequences mentioned in the texts. He suggests that these scholars are referring simply to verses which can be directly derived from the texts.[8] In paragraph 3.4, he mentions the opinion of Abū Manṣūr, who says that it is necessary to know what relates to a legal rule and not the story itself. Al-Shawkānī does not seem to be convinced by this very general statement.

Consequently, Al-Shawkānī attempts to evaluate the knowledge through a number of *hadīth* and starts arguing with opinions of jurists in paragraph four. He begins with the opinion of some jurists who say that knowledge of 500 *hadīths* would be enough to become a *mujtahid*. He reject this vehemently, saying that there are thousands of *hadīths* including a legal rule. Evidently, Al-Shawkānī argues with the balance between existing *hadīths* and the quantity of knowing 500 *hadīths*. In his opinion, a *mujtahid* must know more than 500. As a

---

6 Al-Shawkānī, "*Irshād al-Fuhūl ilā tahqīq al-haqq min 'ilm al-uṣūl*" (Cairo: Dār al-Islām, 1418/1998), 2 vols. Vol. 2, para.3
7 Al-Shawkānī, *loc. cit.*, para. 3.1
8 Al-Shawkānī, *loc. cit.*, para. 3.2

result of this approach, he starts giving opinions of higher requirements. He cites Ibn al-'Arabī, who said that 3000 *hadīths* are necessary and Abū Bakr al-Darīr, who was told by Ahmad b. Hanbal that 500,000 *hadīths* are required.[9] He adds a statement of one of the followers saying that this only applies on the very best jurists and cited Hanbal, who said that there are 1,200 *hadīths* applicable for the derivation of legal rules.[10] By counter-arguing Ahmad b. Hanbals opinion through the relativistic statement of one of his followers, Al-Shawkānī shows his negative stance on the number of 500,000 *hadīths*. Consequently, he moves on to a more abstract approach, saying that it is no condition to know all *hadīths* literally. Instead, a *mujtahid* must be able to gain access to a source of all the *hadīths* relating to a rule, and then perform *ijtihād* by referring to them. All the mentioned scholars agree on this idea.[11] In dispute is the source itself. Al-Ghazālī mentions in this context the *Sunan* of Abū Dāwūd,[12] which is seen as inadequate by other legal scholars. Reasons for that are due to their opinion, missing important *hadīths* and contained faults in this *Sunan*. Al-Shawkānī prefers in this dispute also a general approach rather than following one particular opinion. In his conclusion in paragraph 4.7, he says that a *mujtahid* must be able to assess the trustworthiness and evidence of *hadīths* to filter. He develops this point to the quality of assessment. In his opinion, an important condition of being a *mujtahid* is to check the *isnād* intensely. Al-Shawkānī also concludes, in retrospect of the mentioned debates, that it is more significant for a *mujtahid* to evaluate the importance of a *hadīth* rather than the ability to memorise all of them. In his concluding opinion on this first

---

9 Al-Shawkānī, *loc. cit.*, para. 4.1
10 Al-Shawkānī, *loc. cit.*, para. 4.2
11 Al-Shawkānī, *loc. cit.*, para. 4.3-4.6
12 Al-Shawkānī, *loc. cit.*, para. 4.4

condition, Al-Shawkānī shows his opposing attitude on the restriction of *ijtihād*. He underlines that some requirements of legal scholars are exaggerated and argues for a less strict approach, which would open the door to become a *mujtahid* for a wider circle of jurists.

After the knowledge of the primary texts of Islamic Law, Al-Shawkānī mentions the second condition in paragraph five. In his view, a *mujtahid* "must know the questions regarding *ijmā'*".[13] *Ijmā'*, which means consensus, is the third source of Islamic Law.[14] He does not clarify which questions in connection to *ijmā'* he thinks of. He only gives the reader the reason why, saying that a *mujtahid* must know them to ensure that no given *fatwā* contradicts to the consensus. He adds that there is little decided by consensus that should concern the performer of *ijtihād*, he simplifies the complexity of *ijmā'* through limiting it to few cases. These cases must be known by a *mujtahid*. Regarding the above mentioned function, it is possible to reason that Al-Shawkānī also thinks of questions about how *ijmā'* could be achieved. In my opinion, his second condition includes the knowledge about juristic disagreements, concerning for instance, the questions about which legal scholars should be involved in the consensus geographically and by differing between certain degrees. Furthermore, these debates include, for example, questions about changing disagreements to *ijmā'*, how the scholars should express their agreement and if *ijmā'* is binding cross-generational.[15] Al-Shawkānī requires that a *mujtahid* must know about these questions. He does not postulate a particular view on the questions and consequently, every view is acceptable.

---

13 Al-Shawkānī, *loc. cit.*, para. 5
14 K Vikor, *loc. cit.*, p.78
15 K A El Fadl, *'Speaking in God's Name: Islamic Law, Authority, and Women'* (2001), p.64

His third condition is sufficient knowledge of the Arabic language.[16] A *mujtahid* must be so proficient in his handling of the language that he is able to understand and interpret texts of the *Qur'an* and the *Sunnah*. By means of this ability, he must be skilled to extract legal rules from the texts. Al-Shawkānī takes, again, a moderate approach by excluding the knowledge of the texts by heart and saying that abiding by the positions of the great scholars is an adequate way. This decreases the mental work of prospective *mujtahids*.

The knowledge of *usūl al-fiqh* is the fourth condition a *mujtahid* must control.[17] Al-Shawkānī points out the importance of this capability by calling it "the tent of *ijtihād*" and an "art". The cause of this is that *usūl al-fiqh* is the basis of building a *fatwā* and thus he "must have mastery over it".[18] Consequently, a *mujtahid* is able to clarify disagreements and make conclusions about them. Furthermore, Al-Shawkānī supports his argument with opinions of two jurists, who agree on the importance of *usūl al-fiqh*. It is clear, that Al-Shawkānī does not condone another view on the significance of *usūl al-fiqh* to a *mujtahid*.

The fifth condition to be a *mujtahid* concerns abrogation. To avoid the creation of a *fatwā* on the basis of evidence which has been abrogated, it is obviously necessary to know which verses can be used to compose one. This knowledge is compulsory to avoid failures.

In his last paragraphs, Al-Shawkānī mentions disputed conditions, where

---
16 Al-Shawkānī, *loc. cit.*, para. 6
17 Al-Shawkānī, *loc. cit.*, para. 7
18 Al-Shawkānī, *loc. cit.*, para. 7

legal scholars do not agree if these conditions are a requirement for becoming a *mujtahid*. One of these conditions relates to the inclusion of rational indicators in the wisdom of a legal scholar.[19] Al-Shawkānī militates against the inclusion. It would comprise the indicators of reason in the performance of *ijtihād*. He does not agree with that, because reason is not part of *ijtihād*, in his opinion. This discussion is dominated by the definition of *ijtihād*. Due to different interpretations, some jurists include indicators of reason like al-Ghazālī and al-Rāzī, and some only see the indicators of law included. Al-Shawkānī follows the latter opinion. Astonishing is the fact that Al-Shawkānī disagrees primarily with the great scholar al-Ghazālī in his reasoning after he has supported some of his arguments with al-Ghazālī's statements. That shows clearly, that Al-Shawkānī does not feel obliged to follow one opinion through his reasoning.

Moreover, Al-Shawkānī adds to the discussion, that a *mujtahid* must know the principles of religion.[20] Without clarifying which opinion he prefers, he mentions only the position of al-Āmidī in detail. Consequently, it seems that Al-Shawkānī follows al-Āmidī's position which says that a "*mujtahid* must know necessary truths of religion", but not in every detail. Repeatedly, Al-Shawkānī shows his attitude to a moderate approach for the conditions.

Al-Shawkānī goes on to the question how detailed the knowledge of law should be.[21] Some jurists like al-Ghazālī and Abū Mansūr say that it is a requirement to know the details of law before one can become a *mujtahid*. Again Al-Shawkānī disputes the position of al-Ghazālī by giving a challenging

---
19 Al-Shawkānī, *loc. cit.*, para. 9
20 Al-Shawkānī, *loc. cit.*, para. 10
21 Al-Shawkānī, *loc. cit.*, para. 11

question which assumes a "vicious circle" as result of this strict approach. This rhetorical question indicates the position of Al-Shawkānī.

Al-Shawkānī closes in paragraphs 12 and 13, agreeing that the knowledge of proving the *hadīth* transmitters and performing *qiyās* is very important for being a *mujtahid*. But contrary to other legal scholars, he includes these conditions under *usūl al-fiqh* and does not see them as single conditions.

It appears to me, that Al-Shawkānī does not want to establish too strict requirements on jurists which aspire towards becoming a *mujtahid*. He does not want to make it impossible and, therefore, he prefers a moderate approach concerning the conditions of being a *mujtahid*. This is also reflected by his reasoning in the text. He cites great scholars with partly high and "exaggerated" requirements. But mostly, he disagrees these excessive positions, giving less strict statements of other jurists and shows his positive stance on their arguments. In this connection, Al-Shawkānī does not feel constrained to follow the argumentation of one legal scholar loyallly from the beginning constantly to the end, shown at the example of al-Ghazālī. Nevertheless, Al-Shawkānī requires at the same time in certain conditions, mastery and a sound knowledge. He postulates this especially for the knowledge of the language and for *usūl al-fiqh*, because it is the foundation of Islamic jurisprudence. He concentrates on keeping the conditions high for the capability to work with the texts and extract legal rules, more than learning them by heart. All in all, this text clearly shows Al-Shawkānī's position against an overdrawn restriction and for a greater use of *ijtihād*. Consequently, there are not many conditions which have to be fulfilled to be a *mujtahid*. This makes it not extremely difficult. But certain conditions, like *usūl al-fiqh*, require special qualities in the person. Therefore, not everybody is able to become a *mujtahid*. The text is like a syllabus which tells one how to assess *mujtahids*. Considering that Al-Shawkānī established his reputation partly by defining requirements to attain different scholarly status, this text must be seen as highly significant for prospective and experienced *mujtahids*. It is a crucial instrument to identify a *mujtahid* and to understand their role in Islamic jurisprudence as well as in society.

Bibliography

El Fadl K A, *Speaking in God's Name: Islamic Law, Authority, and Women*
(Oxford: Oneworld Publications, 2001)

Haykel B, *Revival and Reform in Islam: The Legacy of Muhammad al-Shawkānī* (Cambridge: Cambridge University Press, 2003)

Jansen J, Bearman P and others (ed.), *Encyclopaedia of Islam: Second Edition*
(Leiden: E.J. Brill)

Kramer G, Martin R C and others (ed.), *Encyclopedia of Islam and the Muslim World* (New York: Macmillan Reference USA, 2004)

Vikor K, *Between God and the Sultan: A History of Islamic Law*
(London: C. Hurst & Co. LTD., 2005)

YOUR KNOWLEDGE HAS VALUE

- We will publish your bachelor's and master's thesis, essays and papers

- Your own eBook and book - sold worldwide in all relevant shops

- Earn money with each sale

Upload your text at www.GRIN.com and publish for free